Best House

Useful Cleaning & O... ...ps That
Will Make Your Life Easier

Disclaimer and Terms of Use:

Effort has been made to ensure that the information in this book is accurate and complete, however, the author and the publisher do not warrant the accuracy of the information, text and graphics contained within the book due to the rapidly changing nature of science, research, known and unknown facts and internet. The Author and the publisher do not hold any responsibility for errors, omissions or contrary interpretation of the subject matter herein. This book is presented solely for motivational and informational purposes only.

Table of Contents

Introduction

Let's say goodbye to the myth that cleaning the house takes hours and lots of human effort. Most of the household hacks in this report work in a matter of minutes. Moreover, you are no longer required to wage a scrubbing war to clean your countertops or floors. A gentle scrubbing is all that's needed because of the effectiveness of these household hacks. Based on the time requirement for each kind of stain you can come up with an efficient cleaning schedule that lets you clean multiple spots within the same hour.

The hacks presented are absolutely safe for you and your furnishings. However, as with any other cleaning material, some might cause damage to equipment and furniture if not applied correctly. If you are trying a method or using a cleaning ingredient for the first time, proceed with caution and follow the procedures and measurements to the letter. We recommend that you start on a small area to test it out.

Let's get started!

Ingredients

It's important to know the ingredients of a recipe before attempting it, it is important to know the various ingredients that are a part of different household hacks. In this chapter, let's take a look at the various components of the numerous household hacks we'll mention in this book. You'll be happy to know that these ingredients are readily available and are way cheaper than any of your commercial cleaning products.

Rubbing Alcohol

Also known as ethyl alcohol, rubbing alcohol is a well-known solvent. So beware that it can damage your surfaces if you use it in overly generous proportions. What makes it an important ingredient if it is risky to use it? Well, even the toughest of stains will have to kiss your surfaces goodbye - and quickly! - if you clean them with the right proportion of rubbing alcohol.

Mineral Oil

Mineral oil, which is derived from petroleum, is an important ingredient in many skincare products. Mineral oil is capable of removing rust from steel surfaces in an effective fashion. It is also used to polish wooden surfaces.

Dishwashing Liquid

Unlike other commercial cleaning products, dishwashing liquid is fairly safe to use. When used in different combinations with other ingredients, it is capable of removing all kinds of stains. It is a very eco-friendly ingredient despite being a commercial product.

Lemon

Lemon is used in combination with other ingredients like sea salt, rubbing alcohol, and dish washing liquid to tackle different kinds of stains present on various surfaces. In addition to its multiple uses, lemon is very cheap and always available.

Essential Oils

Say no to bad odor with essential oils! Ever wondered how spas are always filled with such pleasant aromas? Well, the answer is essential oils. They are capable of removing bad odors from the various rooms in your house.

Essential oils are nothing but cold pressed oils extracted from flowers and fruits. Some examples of essential oils are clove oil, lavender oil, and eucalyptus oil. They are inexpensive and can do a better job of making your room smell good than an expensive air freshener.

Sea Salt

Sea salt is well known for its absorbent properties. When used with lemon, it can remove tough stains. Apart from absorbing stains, sea salt also absorbs bad odors.

Hydrogen Peroxide

Hydrogen peroxide is a safe and effective bleaching agent (much better than chlorine, in fact). It can be used for bleaching the different surfaces in your home. Apart from that, it can be used to retain the brightness of the white surfaces in your home. It is also an effective disinfectant.

Blotting Paper

Blotting paper is capable of removing even the toughest of oil stains and grime. Always keep some blotting paper handy to remove any oil stains immediately instead of putting it off for another time.

Kitchen

Freshen Up Your Kitchen

The kitchen is one place that should always smell good. Do not buy expensive air fresheners; instead, take your favorite natural scent oils and drip a few drops into some cotton wool balls. Then place the cotton balls in the corners of your kitchen and in the shelves where they are out of sight. This will give the kitchen a beautiful fragrance that will last for weeks.

Sanitize the Kitchen Sink

Research has shown that the kitchen sink contains more germs and bacteria than the toilet seat. It is hard to believe this, but it is true, as the sink is less sanitized than the toilet seat. To start, wash the sink with hot soapy water (or with vinegar). Then spray some hydrogen peroxide into it. This will serve to kill the germs. To give additional sparkle to stainless steel, add some mineral oil after cleaning using a sponge or soft cloth.

Wash Dishes after Dinner

Fill your sink with hot soapy water before sitting down to dinner and soak all dirty utensils not being used at the dinner table. After you finish your dinner, add the dining utensils to make them easier to wash. Never make the mistake of piling up dishes in the sink overnight as this becomes a target for cockroaches and bacteria.

Dirty Sinks

A sink full of grease and grime can be difficult to clean. Try to fill the sink with warm water and vinegar, and then let it soak. After a few minutes, it will be easier to scrub the grease and the grime off. The vinegar loosens up all the grease, saving you precious time. If you want the sink to remain spotless, you should coat it with turtle wax. This will prevent any greasy substances from sticking to it, and it will shine like new all the time.

Some more tips when it comes to cleaning different kinds of sinks are:

Porcelain Sinks

a) Stains on the surfaces of porcelain sinks can be removed by pouring a mixture of half a cup of dishwashing liquid diluted by half a cup of water on the surface. Let it stay on the surface for around ten minutes and scrub it off.

b) A combination of coarse salt and hydrogen peroxide can be used to remove tough stains from the surface.

c) The drain can be cleaned with the help of a mixture of hydrogen peroxide and baking soda.

Stainless Steel Sinks

a) Sprinkle some baking powder on the dry surface. Scrub it after five minutes. This ought to keep your sink shining and clean.

b) A mixture of coarse salt and lemon juice ought to remove any stains. Sprinkle the salt and squeeze the lemon juice over the salt. Scrub it off using a toothbrush.

Microwave

Prepare a combination of water and vinegar as for the sink and heat it up in the microwave. This will help loosen any stuck food particles. Vinegar also removes unpleasant smells which may linger in the microwave.

You can also try adding four tablespoons of lemon juice to a cup of water and heating it in the microwave for five minutes. This should be done in an open bowl to allow the steam to condense on the inside of the microwave. Afterwards, wipe with a clean, dry cloth.

An added bonus: after cleaning your microwave, you can use the heated water and vinegar to clean garbage disposal bins or the sink.

Microwave Your Sponges

After you finish doing the dishes at night, microwave the sponges for a few minutes to kill all the germs.

Cooking Pots

Cooking pots are one of the toughest items in the kitchen to wash due to food residues, grease, and gunk. To save time and energy cleaning one, pour some water and soap into the pot and bring it to a boil. Let it cool, and leave it for a few more minutes for the toughest dirt. The grease should come off easier afterwards. You can also add some baking soda to ease the process.

Blender

If you need to clean your blender quickly and effectively, fill it with water and add a few drops of dishwashing soap. Turn the blender on and let it wash itself. Rinse it and you're done. If you blended something that left a smell, add a few drops of vanilla or lemon to the water then turn it once to shake the mixture around the surface.

Unpleasant Dishwasher Smell

Dishwashers can acquire an odor after a few cycles of use. To get rid of it, remove any food items from the bottom of the dishwasher then put some lemon Kool-Aid in the detergent slot. This will do the trick. Aim to wash the dishwasher at least once a month to avoid accumulation of streaks and debris.

Coffee Maker

There are times that our coffee does not taste very fresh, and sometimes this is due to the coffee maker being not very clean. Coffee makers can be difficult to clean because not all the areas are easily accessible. Put a mixture of vinegar and water into the coffee maker and run it for a few minutes. To avoid a vinegar taste in your coffee after the wash, run some fresh water through the coffee maker a few times. Clean the coffee maker regularly to avoid buildup of grime.

As you will probably have noticed, vinegar is a very important ingredient in most cleaning processes, so have it ready. It will do the trick for getting rid of bad smells in most household items. Charcoal too absorbs odors, especially in larger items such as fridges.

Rust on Kitchen Items

Items such as cutlery and knives will usually rust when left in damp conditions. To get rid of the rust, take a potato, cut it in half, apply baking soda to the exposed part of the potato, and scrub on the rusty surface of the knife. This will immediately get rid of all the rust.

Measuring Cups

Measuring cups can get sticky if used to measure substances such as honey and jelly. To avoid this, coat the measuring cup with olive oil along the surface before use. This will prevent the substances from sticking to the cup.

Vegetable Odors

Vegetable odors are unavoidable in the kitchen, but you can minimize them by placing newspapers in the shelves and drawers. The newspapers not only make the shelves easy to clean but actually absorb most of the vegetable odor.

Barbecue Grates

BBQ grates can prove to be a real headache if you let them cool down, so the best way to wash them is while they are still hot. Immediately when you finish barbecuing, wash the grates and store them, otherwise the grease will congeal and it will be harder and more time-consuming to wash them. There are some special washing brushes for cleaning BBQ grates, but you could still buy a normal hard bristle brush and use it for this job.

Blocked Drains

A blocked drain in the kitchen or anywhere else in the house will easily be cleared by applying a mixture of water, baking soda and vinegar, then rinsing with hot water. This will unblock the drain. Use this procedure regularly even when drains are not blocked, as it clears any buildup from the drain.

Insects and Cockroaches

Cockroaches can be a menace and are extremely difficult to control. There are some chemicals that can get rid of them, but these can pose a risk to pets and kids. If you want to safely get rid of them, use cucumber skins. Place these skins where the roaches are commonly found. They don't like them and will disappear.

Gasoline and Other Smells in Your Home

In the kitchen and around the house, you may find some really upsetting smells. It could be pet's vomit or even gasoline. Whenever gasoline has come in contact with your home furnishings or flooring you will experience its strong, unpleasant smell. This is very disturbing in a home setting, and the bad thing is it doesn't easily go away on its own and can stick around for days. Water and soap will never get rid of this smell; you actually need an odor fighting solution. Once again, vinegar comes to the rescue.

Vinegar is a very strong odor fighting agent due to its acidic properties. Vinegar is also readily available and you'll find it in most homes. Vanilla and lemon are good alternatives. These three items have been referred to as "natural deodorizers" and can be used around the home to fight any odor, not just that of gasoline, to good effect.

Really Stubborn Stains

If you are getting rid of really stubborn stains, such as tough dirt, burnt-on grease, and grime, you need to have a steam cleaner. This is because the dirt and the grease, when left in the kitchen for a long time, becomes a haven for bacteria which in turn can lead to food poisoning. This is mostly in ovens and on stoves, but other surfaces may also need this attention. If all other tips aren't working, purchase a steam cleaner.

The good thing about a steam cleaner is that it doesn't actually require a cleaning agent to work.

Just add water and it will get rid of even the most stubborn stains. The steam cleaner is a vital cleaning tool, especially for people with larger households. Regarding power use, you do not need to worry about this as they don't consume a lot of electricity. They are generally very efficient and anyway you only need to use them for the most stubborn stains.

Wash Around in a Circle

When washing the kitchen, do it in a circle. Begin with the area around the stove and move clockwise round the kitchen. You might ask why. It's because the area near the stove is the dirtiest and contains a lot of grease which shouldn't be spread to other areas of the kitchen.

Cabinets

It is very easy for your kitchen cabinets to get dirty and for grime to develop on the surfaces of the cabinets. The grimy surfaces of the cabinets attract fur, hair and other dust particles. This not only gives your cabinet a gross look but also makes it an unhygienic piece of furniture in your kitchen. Don't fret. Grime can be easily removed from the cabinet surfaces by cleaning them with a mixture of mineral oil and baking soda. You can also apply a mixture of mineral oil, dishwashing liquid and coarse salt on the surfaces to get rid of the grime.

It is not only important that your cabinets look lustrous; the insides should be clean as well. A mixture of lemon juice and coarse salt can be used to clean the interiors of the cabinets. The lemon juice is effective in removing old and dried stains while the coarse salt is capable of chipping away the stains.

Countertops

It is important that you keep your countertops clean because that is where you do most of your prep work before cooking. Here are some tips to keep your countertops clean:

a) Remove any rust that has developed on the countertops by cleaning them with a cloth dipped in a mixture of warm water and alcohol, combined in equal proportions. The alcohol will remove the rust and disinfect the countertops.

b) Bad odors from the countertops can be taken care of by cleaning them with a cloth dipped in a mixture of half a cup of baking soda and two cups of water.

c) Granite countertops can lose their luster quickly. A good way to ensure that your granite countertops retain their shiny luster is by scrubbing them regularly with alcohol. This not only removes stains but also keeps them lustrous.

Bathroom

Put a Second Shower Rod in the Back of Your Shower

Looking for more hanging space? Consider placing another tension rod at the back of your bathtub shower. Add a few hooks and you have additional storage for loofahs, sponges, washcloths and other items. You can even get small plastic bins and baskets to hang on the rod.

Clean Up the Toilet with Coke

Want to get rid of those stains that hang around? Pour a bottle of coke into the toilet bowl. When you pour, make sure that you pour around the rim as well. Leave the coke to sit for an hour or so. The enzymes and chemicals in the coke should remove all the stains. If you have some stains left, attack with a toilet brush and then flush. Flush a couple times to get rid of the sugar, especially if you live in a buggy area.

Use Essential Oils to Deodorize

Essential oils are easy to find at most natural food and grocery stores. Essential oils make your bathroom smell fresh and clean naturally. Instead of chemical fresheners, choose the natural oil of your choice. When in doubt, lavender, lemon, and orange are always good choices. Put a few drops inside your toilet paper roll and in the bathroom trash can, for starters.

Clean Bathroom Grout Naturally

Want to clean and avoid mildew? Spray Vodka or alcohol on your bathroom caulk. Let it sit for no more than five minutes and mix well. You can also clean grout by mixing baking soda and water into a paste and putting it down on the dirty grout. Spray with a vinegar and water solution (the baking soda will foam) and then rinse away with warm water. To prevent grout from staining, spray with white vinegar and wipe once every week or so.

Shine Bathroom Porcelain with Baby Oil

A few drops of baby oil or other oil can shine porcelain. Use this method to shine up toilet and sink areas, but avoid the bathtub. Add a few drops of baby oil to a cloth. Buff the toilet or sink until it feels dry and watch it shine up. Remember, only a drop or so of oil is needed.

Clean Shower Doors with a Dryer Sheet

Used dryer sheets have multiple uses around the home, from dusting to scrubbing. Save dryer sheets in a bin in the laundry room so you have them on hand for household use. To clean your shower doors use this hack. Put a few drops of water on the used dryer sheet and scrub the shower door, watching it clean up quickly.

Make a Natural Tub and Tile Cleaner

You need a large bowl for mixing the solution and a spray bottle. Mix 3/4 cup baking soda, 1/4 cup lemon juice, 3 tablespoons of salt, 3 tablespoons of dishwashing liquid, 1/2 cup vinegar and 10 drops essential oil if desired. Shake and spray a small amount, and then wipe, rinse and wipe again.

Prevent Mildew on Shower Curtains by Pre-Soaking

Don't wait for shower curtains to get moldy. Use an ounce of prevention instead. Place a new shower curtain in the bathtub with water and about 1/4 cup of regular salt. Let soak for three hours. Rinse if desired and hang. The salt will act as a protective barrier.

Clean Your Shower Head with Vinegar

Save time and energy. You can clean your shower head without removing it, or spending long amounts of time with your arms above your head. Grab a large baggie or Ziploc bag and add white vinegar. Put the baggie over the showerhead and tie it in place. Leave it at least overnight. Remove the bag, and run the shower in the morning.

Use Baking Soda to Clean Drains

Bathroom drains tend to need some maintenance every so often. Shampoo, soap, hair and other particles get into drains no matter how small the holes. Cleaning your drain on a regular basis will keep things running smoothly. Pour a half cup of baking soda directly into the drain. Add a small amount of hot water to make sure that it all goes down the drain. Let sit for a few hours, and then rinse with more hot water, making sure all the soda is washed away.

Clean Bathroom Mold with Bleach

Depending on your climate, you may have tough mold issues. Keeping mold at bay is a health issue as well as a visual one. Fill a spray bottle with a cup of bleach, a half a cut of detergent add hot water to the top of the bottle. Spray on moldy areas. Leave for one hour then rinse well. Repeat as needed. Remember when mixing bleach to gently pour bleach into other liquids to avoid splashing.

Clean Bathroom Toys Naturally

Fill a clean bucket with warm water and half a cup to a cup of vinegar. Add bathtub and other toys and allow to soak for ten minutes. Wash gently with a sponge or towel and lay out to dry. No rinsing is necessary.

Clean the Floor Around the Toilet

Anyone who lives with, or has boys knows about toilet bowl over spray. Get rid of the "boy bathroom smell" with natural ingredients. Mix baking soda and lemon juice until it's thick and pourable like a batter. Put the paste all on the floor around the toilet and on the toilet seat. Leave the paste for fifteen minutes, come back and spray with white vinegar (it will foam up). When the solution is done foaming, clean with a wet cloth until all of the residue is gone.

Keep Your Bathroom Mirror from Fogging Up

Are you tired of wiping the fog and steam off bathroom mirrors? Cover your mirror with shaving cream, and then wipe off with a towel. This method should keep your mirror free for a month with regular use. Simple and effective.

Put a Small Magnet Strip on the Inside of your Medicine Cabinet

Get a magnetic strip or small magnets that you can mount inside your bathroom cabinet, or in another workable place. The magnet will help you corral small metal items such as hair clips, metal tweezers and other loose bathroom items.

For Really Deep Cleaning Projects, Use your Drill

Did you know you can get a scrub brush attachment for most household drills? Save on the elbow grease and muscle power when spring cleaning. Use the cleaner of your choice and your drill with scrub brush to clean tile walls and floors, bathroom stains and more.

Use Clear Nail Polish to Eliminate Stains

Ever notice how shaving cans and other items end up leaving rust marks on your shelves and medicine cabinet? Grab some clear nail polish and cover the bottom of the cans and let dry. No more stains on shelves, tubs or shower racks.

Remove Hairspray From Bathroom Walls

If you spray your hair regularly in the bathroom, residue ends up on the walls. Remove it by making a mixture of one part water and two parts rubbing alcohol. Add a few drops of dishwashing liquid. Spray the solution on your walls and wipe clean. Note: use this hack for vinyl walls or gloss paint, but not flat paint.

Unplug Your Toilet Without a Plunger

Sometimes you need to unplug a toilet immediately, especially if it's the only toilet available. Don't panic if a plunger is not available. Squirt 1/4 to 1/2 cup of dish soap into the toilet and allow it to sit for 15 minutes. The dish soap will lubricate the pipe and settle at the bottom of the toilet. Follow this up with a pot of boiling water, and then flush normally.

Kill Mildew Naturally

Kill mildew with a bleach solution. Mix one part bleach to ten parts water and spray the affected area. Clean with a soft brush or sponge. The diluted solution is strong enough to clean mildew and yet mild enough that it will not discolor clothes or surfaces. Pour the bleach into the water to avoid splashing.

Scrub Your Bathtub with Baking Soda

Mix a teaspoon of liquid soap to a cup of baking soda. Add a little water to make a paste, and essential oil if desired. Scrub your bathtub normally with this solution. Your bathtub will sparkle and smell great!

Make Your Own Deodorizing Discs

These discs are easy to make and great for diaper pails, trash cans, trash compactors and more. Start with a bowl and a small mold (a silicone mold or mini muffin pan). Mix 2 cups baking soda, 1 or two cups distilled water (or boil water for ten minutes), and a few drops of essential oil (lavender or citrus). Pour 1/2 cup of water and the essential oil into the baking soda. Add water as needed to make a thick paste. Divide the mixture equally between your molds or muffin cups. Let dry for at least 24 hours and up to 48 hours until completely dry. Length of time will depend on your climate. Place wherever needed. Discs should last up to a month at least.

Living Room

Clean Microfiber Furniture with Rubbing Alcohol

Fill a spray bottle with alcohol. Saturate the fabric in the area of the stain. Use a white sponge or cloth to scrub the area (colored cloths may release dyes on your couch). Clean the sponge/cloth as necessary. Let the fabric dry completely and re-fluff the fiber. Furniture will look like new!

Use Sharpie Pens to Cover Marks on Furniture

Have a small scratch in your coffee table? Do the legs on your furniture have scratches? Use a Permanent felt tip marker to even out and cover scratches easily. Sharpie actually makes some wood stain colored markers just for this purpose, but there are so many color options you should have no problem matching your furniture. If you are patching the legs, make sure the carpet or floor around the furniture piece is well protected.

Cover Leather Scratch Marks with Shoe Polish

Leather can show scratches fairly easily and mar your beautiful room. Get some shoe polish in a color that matches your leather and use a clean cloth to buff your furniture with the shoe polish. The polish will cover any marks and shine up your leather. Make sure to buff until the cloth comes clean. At that point the shoe polish will be set and clothing should be safe.

Deodorize your Furniture with Baking Soda

Cloth furniture can absorb odors and sweat. Keep them clean and fresh. Grab some baking soda and sprinkle all over the sofa or chair. Leave the baking soda to sit an hour or so and then vacuum the baking soda off the couch. Your couch will be clean, fresh and odor free.

Remove Dog Hair with a Squeegee

Unfortunately, vacuuming does not always pick up all the dog hair on carpets and furniture. Use a window squeegee to help remove dog hair. Choose a long handled model if possible. Roll the rubber portion of the squeegee across the carpet. The rubber will loosen the dog hair. Afterwards, pick up all the clumps of hair easily and then vacuum.

Use Your Vacuum to Deodorize your Living Room

Freshen your living room naturally with essential oils. Soak a cotton ball with your fragrance of choice and then put the cotton ball in the vacuum bag. Start vacuuming. The vacuum will release the essential oil smell while you are cleaning your floors leaving your house smelling clean and natural. You can also get the same effect by putting a cotton ball in an unobtrusive location such as under your furniture or behind the television.

Clean Your TV with Dryer Sheets

Modern TV screens are sensitive and using traditional cleaning methods are not advised. Paper towels, napkins or Kleenex should never be used to clean a flat screen TV. A dryer sheet will remove dust from your television. Another method is to use a microfiber cloth to gently wipe the television.

If using a cloth or a dryer sheet do not remove all the dirt, then try adding a little water to the cloth. Try with another micro fiber cloth. Always use an extremely light touch with your flat screen. Never put water directly on the flat screen, and always clean and dust your flat screen TV with the power off to the TV and all accessories.

Use Baskets to Keep Your Living Room Organized

These days the living room gets used for many different things. We watch TV, using multiple remote controls. We read, we sew, we play games, we do homework and more. Organize all these items with a few pretty baskets. Baskets can be found cheaply at thrift and craft stores, and they keep items "stowed" but still accessible. Keep a basket near the TV with remotes and TV cleaning cloth, for example. A long or square basket on the coffee table can hold pens, reading material and cards. Another advantage of these baskets is that if the occasion arises you can remove those things from the room quickly without doing the "bend and reach" multiple times.

Keep Carpets Smelling Good with Cornstarch

Instead of using a high priced carpet freshener, simply sprinkle cornstarch over your carpet to remove smells. Let the cornstarch sit on the carpet for half an hour and then vacuum as you normally would to pick up the entire cornstarch.

Don't go to Bed with Mugs on the Table

For most of us, nothing is more depressing than getting out of bed and seeing dirty coffee cups, snack dishes and leftover newspapers thrown around the living room. Take five minutes before bed to take the dishes to the kitchen sink, throw out the trash, and put everything else in those storage baskets or bins. You will thank yourself in the morning.

Throw a T-shirt over a Broom for Dusting

Especially in the living room, dusting is not just about tables and shelves. There are cobwebs in the corners, dust behind the entertainment stand and more. While some vacuums have long reaching attachments, often times we have to fake it. By putting an old T-shirt on a broom, you should be able to reach most cracks, crevices and high places in your living room. It's a low cost solution and the T-shirt can then be washed and even worn again.

Rotate Cushions and Pillows

Couch cushions. Pillows and throw pillows will stay fresher and plumper if rotated. Most couch cushions have a zipper in the back, but do allow for rotating from top to bottom every so often. Make sure to plump and dust when you rotate. Unless throw pillows get full wear, rotate them as well. You may want to consider having a second cover for your throw pillows so they can be washed.

Clean Vomit off Furniture with Baking Soda

Admittedly this is something most of us would not like to hear about - until the day we need it. But when we need it, we need it. Clean off excess vomit and make a paste of baking soda and water. Put mixture all over the area. Spread with a spatula like frosting. Wait twelve hours or until the consistency is a powder again. Vacuum and vacuum a second time if needed.

Remove Pet Stains with Vinegar and Water

Anyone who has ever adopted a puppy or had sick animals knows about the dangers of pet stains, especially on the carpet. Mix 2 cups white vinegar, 2 cups warm water, and 4 tablespoons of baking soda. If the stain is still wet, soak up as much extra liquid as possible. Do this by putting paper towels or cloths on the stain and pressing down firmly (use an old shoe or book if needed). Otherwise you have the danger of the pee going through to the floor or the pad. Do not spot the stain until all the liquid possible has been removed.

Once you have finished the first step, make the solution above. There will be fizzing when you add the baking soda. Either pour or spray the cleaner onto the stain, wait five minutes, and. begin blotting. If necessary, follow up with the same solution without the baking soda. Continue blotting until dry. Use cornstarch prior to vacuuming for the next few vacuums to insure there are no residual odors.

Clothing

Let Hairspray be Your Friend

Keep hairspray on hand to for emergency stain removal. In this case, we mean the old fashioned hair spray, like Aqua Net, not hair gel. Spray the ink spot or other affected area. Allow to sit for thirty minutes and blot with a damp cloth. Repeat as necessary. Hairspray will also remove lipstick stains in the same manner.

Use Shampoo as a Pre-Soak

Shampoo is a great degreaser and can remove some of the worst stains. Pour or squirt a small amount on the stained area and spread it around. Let it sit for ten minutes and then wash the clothing as usual.

Use Hydrogen Peroxide for Blood Stains

Before any stain removal product, rinse the blood stained fabric in COLD water using a little soap. If there is still blood on the garment, pour hydrogen peroxide all over the area and allow it to sit for several minutes. Rinse with cold water. Repeat if needed then wash the garment normally.

Use Rubbing Alcohol to Remove Paint

When it comes to acrylic paint or nail polish, rubbing alcohol is your solution. Saturate the stain with rubbing alcohol. Then use your fingernail to scratch off the paint. When the paint or nail polish is mainly gone, wash the fabric normally,

Use Cornstarch to Get Rid of Grease and Oil

Clean grease and oil before washing. Oil tends to repel water, meaning that soapy water is not of much help until after most of the grease is removed. Sprinkle cornstarch on the stain and allow it to sit for fifteen minutes. Scrape off the cornstarch and then dab with a damp towel or sponge.

Refresh Suede Shoes with an Emery Board

Gently rub an emery board across the suede nap to remove spots and renew the nap.

Use Shaving Cream to Remove Makeup Stains

You need a damp cloth and shaving cream. Spread the shaving cream with the cloth over the stained area. Put the garment in the washer and clean as usual. If the item in question is not washable, rinse in the sink and hang to dry.

Use the Shortest Cycle Possible on Your Washer and Dryer

This may take some trial and error to figure out, and may depend on the type of clothing. However, the shorter the wash and dry cycle, the less chance for clothes to fade or wear out early and you save on energy.

Read the Instructions on Your Clothing

Manufacturers are required to put clothing care instructions in all clothing. The best way to keep your clothing well cared for is to follow the instructions to the maximum level. If you want to push the envelope, do it with something inexpensive or that you are not attached to.

Add Vinegar to the Wash to Brighten Clothing

White vinegar is mild enough that it will not harm your clothing, but acidic enough that it will remove the residue from soaps and fabric softeners from your clothing. Add one half cup to the final rinse and see clothes look fresh and brighter.

Have a Basket or Bin for Clothing That Can't be Dried

Put it in your closet or above the washer and dryer or a place that works for you. By having a basket specifically for delicate clothing, you don't have to worry about sorting clothing out before they dry and your chances of shrinking something are much lower.

Clean Yellow Sweat Stains off Clothing

Yellow stains on clothing means that sweat has set into the fabric. Make clothes clean again by rubbing the stains with a mixture of one part dish soap and two parts hydrogen peroxide. Let sit for a couple of hours, then rinse the stains and wash normally.

Make Your Own Dryer Sheets

Homemade dryer sheets are less toxic and more eco-friendly, as well as cheaper than store bought. Like store bought, they can be used many times. You'll need a Mason or other sealable jar, 1/2 cup vinegar, and eight drops essential oil (tee tree oil is a mild scent), and your choice of cotton cloths. T-shirts or cheap towels from the dollar store work best. Cut your towels into small pieces. Put the vinegar and the oil into a small bowl and mix. Pour into the jar over the cut cloths. Seal and invert a couple times. Remove a cloth section, squeeze excess liquid and throw into the dryer with your clothes.

Laundry

Keep Your Washing Machine Clean

Whether you have a front loader or a top loading machine, washing machines tend to collect dirt and gunk. Remove all the debris from the seal and lint catcher area first. Then run the washing machine on warm or hot with a solution of equal amounts baking soda and white vinegar.

Clean your Dryer Duct to be Safe

Many households experience a fire as a result of dirty dryer exhaust ducts. Protect your household by cleaning out the dryer duct as part of your annual maintenance. You could pay a professional, however you can clean this on our own in just a few minutes. Turn off and unplug your dryer before doing anything else, and if you have a gas dryer, turn off the gas. Remove the lint trap and clean the screen. Run a cleaning brush along the lint trap to catch everything. Finally, clean up loose lint with your vacuum.

Once the lint trap is clean, pull the dryer away from the wall and unscrew or unclamp the hoses from either end. Use the vacuum to clean out all the duct parts. Clean the space behind your dryer as well. Reattach the hoses with screws or a clamp, making sure the seal is tight so no lint gets out behind the dryer.

Store Clothing Vertically so it is Easier to See

Putting your clothing in drawers horizontally (in a stack) means that you need to paw through the piles to pull something. It also means you don't have the best view of your clothing when trying to choose an outfit. By folding and arranging your clothing vertically, your clothing looks neat and organized. You'll also be able to see and pull out your garments with ease.

Reverse Your Laundry Room Shelving

If you reverse hang your metal laundry room shelves, they will hang at a small angle, with the front of the shelves being lower than the back. Place small bins or laundry baskets on top of the shelves. It will be easy to sort in between loads, and the baskets will be easier to reach.

Corral Missing Socks with Clothes Pins

Hang a piece of thin rope or a laundry line on one wall of your laundry room. Attach clothes pins. Whenever there is an unmatched sock, hang it on the line. Eventually, matches should appear and then be returned to their rightful owners.

Use a Ladder for a Drying Rack

If your laundry room is simply too small for a drying rack, consider hanging one from the ceiling. Use an old wooden ladder and hang it from the ceiling with chains (be sure to secure ceiling studs). Add some hooks and hangers and you have a place to hang those items that are better air dried.

Use a Drink Dispenser for Laundry Detergent

Stores such as Walmart, Target and the dollar store regularly have plastic drink dispensers with spigots (especially in the warm months) for lemonade and tea. Fill a dispenser with detergent and place it on the rack above your washer and dryer. Use a measuring cup or jelly jar when dispensing the detergent. This eliminates mess and having to lift heavy detergent bottles.

Garage

The garage is the last place we think of when cleaning our homes. It is often assumed that the garage is just somewhere to store everything that can't fit in the house. This is wrong: The garage also needs attention, and it is not all that hard to do it.

First, organize the garage so that items are not strewn all over. If something is not needed anymore, don't let it sit there; rather, give it away or sell it if it is still usable. If it is not, then dispose of it properly.

Put your garden tools in one place as you would with any other category of item. The garage floor tends to get a lot of dirt from outside, so use heavy-duty mops and brooms to sweep routinely. The walls will often become stained due to fumes from the car, so a new coat of paint once in a while will keep the garage looking fresh and clean.

Oil stains are another problem. Often we neglect them for so long that they become a problem when you decide to clean up. Wipe off the oil stains from the garage floors with a dry towel as soon as you change the oil in your car. It's a lot easier to remove them immediately than after they've had a chance to soak in. Another way of removing oil stains is to put a blotting paper on top of them and run a hot iron over it. The heat will liquefy the oil and the blotting paper will absorb it. You can also sprinkle some talcum powder on top of oil spills and vacuum it immediately to prevent stains from forming.

Most other stains in the garage can be removed easily by cleaning them with a mixture of warm water and alcohol. You can get rid of the rust stains on your garage tools with a sponge dipped in this mixture, which also cleans them.

Grease stains on the floors and walls of the garage can be removed easily by rubbing some mineral oil over them. The mineral oil loosens the grease, thereby making it easy to wipe off with a dry towel.

The musty smell characteristic of garages occurs because we usually keep our garages closed and there aren't any windows to let in the fresh air that would remove bad odors. But worry not, for you can easily get rid of this musty odor. Mix half a cup of baking soda with two cups of water. When you clean your garage with this mixture, it not only removes the stains but also gets rid of the bad odors.

Alternatively, you can keep a bowl of coffee powder in the center of the garage. This will absorb the bad odors and fill your garage with a rich aroma at the same time. You can also prepare your own room freshener by mixing twenty drops of lavender oil or any other essential oil in half a liter of water and spraying it inside the garage to make it smell fresh.

Mix essential oils, lemon juice, warm water and rubbing alcohol and mop the garage floors with this mixture to get rid of tough stains. The essential oils will also make your floors smell fresh.

Garden

The beauty of a garden can be lost if it is not maintained well. Good maintenance is also necessary to ensure the growth of your plants. If you do not invest some time in your garden, you might as well go ahead and put out a welcome sign for the pests, weeds, and bugs that will surely come to call.

Pests can be one of the biggest problems when you have a garden, and it's hard to know which brand of pesticide to buy. Even the expensive ones are made of chemicals with worrying side effects. But you can let go of all those petty worries by making your own pesticide with natural ingredients that are both effective and eco friendly. Mix some Neem oil with water and detergent. Spray it over the plants. Say goodbye to pests.

If there is a pond in your garden, then make sure you remove the leaves that have accumulated on its surface. Make sure no algae accumulate in the corners.

Water leaking from potted plants can spoil the way your garden looks and make it inconvenient to walk around all the puddles. An easy way to avoid this is by keeping plates under your potted plants. The water will stay in these plates and you can empty them when they get full. But make sure you empty them often; otherwise, the stagnant water can become the breeding ground of numerous disease-bearing mosquitoes. Apart from this, you can also line the plates with sponge balls, which will quickly absorb the water leaking from the plants. Remove these sponge balls from time to time and replace them with fresh ones. Old newspapers will work for this, too.

Weeds can be another issue when you have a garden. An easy way to get rid of them is to spray a mixture of alcohol and water directly on their roots. This will take care of the weeds and prevent them from growing back. Be careful to not spray it on plants you want to keep.

Potted plants can make your garden look beautiful. So it is important that these pots be cleaned from time to time. You can clean them by scrubbing them with a mixture of baking soda and water. If the stains on a pot are too tough to come off with just the scrubbing, dip the pot in a mixture containing 10 percent bleach and 90 percent water. Let it soak in the mixture for around half an hour. Then soak it in clean water for another half an hour. Pat it dry with a clean cloth.

Garden Tools

Proper maintenance of garden tools is as important as maintaining your garden. Clean garden tools are vital for the healthy growth of plans as well as personal hygiene.

Make sure you sterilize your garden tools at regular intervals. These can be done by dipping the garden tools in a tub filled with hot water and dishwashing liquid or rubbing alcohol. If you do not have rubbing alcohol or dishwashing liquid, add black tea to the hot water in the tub. That ought to do the job as well.

Rust is the most important enemy of garden tools. If left unchecked, rust can corrode most of the surface of your garden tools, rendering them useless. To get rid of the rust, immerse the tools in a tub containing oil. Let the tools stay immersed in the tub for at least two days, then remove the tools from the tub and scrub them well.

Another way of removing rust from tools is by immersing them in a bucket full of strong black tea. Make sure the tea is cool before you pour it into a bucket. Let the tools stay immersed in the bucket for some time. The rust will fall apart automatically. Wipe the tools dry with a clean cloth after you remove them from the bucket.

Sharpen the edges of garden tools from time to time with a nail file.

Storing your garden tools properly is very important too. Lay the tools in oiled sand or hang them neatly on pegs.

Miscellaneous Household Hacks

The Best Defense is an Offense

One of the very best ways to keep your house clean is to clean up after yourself, and do small things in short pieces of time. For example, if you include putting your cleaning solution in the toilet and swishing it as part of your morning routine, your bathroom will stay clean longer. By taking this step and wiping down your sink every night with a reusable wipe, you may have to "clean your bathroom" in total less often. If part of your after dinner routine is to clean cooking spots of the stove and wipe down your sink, your kitchen will stay fresher longer. In other words, lots of little steps done in short periods of time can eliminate or at least put off some of those deep cleaning type chores.

Clean Oily Carpet Stains with Baking Soda

Before paying for an expensive service or renting a machine, try this trick: Sprinkle baking soda over the stained area and allow to set ten minutes. Vacuum up the baking soda and vacuum the rest of the carpet as you normally would. For the final step, combine two cups of water, a tablespoon of vinegar and a tablespoon of dishwashing detergent. Sponge into the stained area and allow to sit. Remove the solution with a clean, damp sponge.

Use a Sock to Clean Blinds and other Surfaces

Save all those old socks, holes and all. When it comes time to clean your blinds, make a solution of 1/2 cup vinegar and 1/2 cup water. Slide on the socks, one on each hand. Dip one sock into the solution and then swipe down each blind slat. Use the other sock to dry each of the blind slats. Socks also work well for serious dusting. Spray dusting spray onto the sock and then dust drawers and other small areas easily and quickly. This is a great job to give a child, assuming there are no breakable items at his or her eye level.

Dust Your Keyboard with an Old Toothbrush

Computer keyboards get dirtier easier than almost anything else in the house. Get a clean toothbrush and use it to brush around and under the keys until all the dust and grime is removed.

Ready to De-clutter a Closet? Turn the Clothing Backwards

This tip is an easy method that allows you to see what of your clothing you use regularly. Turn all the hangers so that they are facing backwards. Anytime you remove an item and return it after washing, turn the hangar around the other way. Eventually you'll know which clothes you may want to consider donating.

To remove dust and hair from your lampshades, use a lint roller. Roll it over the lampshade. It will pick up dirt, hair, dust and other residue.

Dust with Dryer Sheets

Dryer sheets can grab dust and keep dust from gathering in the future. Use dryer sheets (new or used) to clean dust of all areas of your home. Baseboards, walks and other areas will clean up immediately. The sheets will increase the time needed between dustings.

Make Your Own Powdered Cleanser

This all-purpose powdered cleanser recipe is easy to use. Sprinkle on damp surface, leave it to work, come back and rinse or wipe clean. Mix 2 cups borax, one cup baking soda, 1/2 cup citric acid, 1/2 cup coarse salt, and essential oil of your choice. Mix well in a bowl and then store in a jar of shaker bottle. Borax is a natural ingredient but should not be left near kids or pets.

Make Your Own Goo Gone (Adhesive Remover)

This solution is great for removing labels from cans, jars or other items as well as taking care of gum and other messes. Mix one part baking soda to two parts vegetable oil. Add orange essential oil to help degrease and add scent. Mix ingredients together in a small bowl. Remove as much of the label as possible. Next, rub the goo gone into the label with your fingers until all the adhesive is gone. Wash normally. Leftover homemade goo gone can be stored in a small jar.

Clean Your Car Headlights with Toothpaste

Dirt, grime, sleet and snow can all work to make your headlights foggy. Sometimes you want better vision but don't have time to hit the car wash. Take a dry cloth and squeeze out some toothpaste. Rub the headlight until grime and gunk are gone. Rinse and dry with a clean cloth.

Clean and Sanitize Ear Buds with Rubbing Alcohol

Ear buds get a lot of use. Cleaning them every so often will protect your ears, sanitize and more. Simply dip a cotton ball into rubbing alcohol and run over the ear buds. Use just a tiny amount of alcohol.

Clean Your Mattress with Vodka

We may not be able to wash our mattresses but we can certainly clean them. Fill a spray bottle with vodka and add the essential oil of your choice. Spray your mattress very lightly and leave to dry. The alcohol kills odors and disinfects, while the essential oil refreshes your bedroom.

Clean Ceiling Fans Using a Pillow Case

Ceiling fans are difficult to clean, especially the top portion of the blades. If your ceiling fan is within reach, simply put a pillow case over each fan blade and remove-taking the dust as you go. This method will eliminate having dust all over the floor (as well as your hair and clothing).

Clean up Broken Glass with Bread

Sometimes when a glass item breaks it can be difficult to find all the small pieces. Grab a piece of bread and begin pressing on counter, floor or surface where there are glass shards. The bread should pick up even the smallest glass pieces while saving you from bending or cutting fingers.

Get Rid of Spiders Naturally

At the first sign of spiders, try this spray repellent. Mix a cup of vinegar, a cup of cayenne pepper, a teaspoon of oil and liquid soap. Mix into a spray bottle. Spray around the door and window entrances. You may want to repeat after it rains. Another solution is to wash your floors with vinegar and water.

Make Your Own Wood Dusting Spray

Easy to make from convenient ingredients, this spray works on most surfaces. Mix the following ingredients in a spray bottle and keep handy for all your dusting needs: 2 tablespoons of olive oil, 1/4 cup of vinegar, 1 3/4 cup of water, and 1/2 teaspoon of lemon (or other) essential oil.

Make Your Own Car Air Freshener

This is a completely simple idea that allows you to choose your own scents. Just buy some wool felt at a craft store for a few scents, punch a hole, attach ribbon and use essential oils of your choice. Experiment with the scents, mixing peppermint and rosemary or vanilla and lemon. If you want your art to imitate life, cut out a green tree and use peppermint or pine scent.

Make a Natural Window Cleaner

Instead of buying window cleaner, make this natural recipe and put it in a spray bottle. Mix 1/4 cup vinegar, 1/4 cup rubbing alcohol, 1 tablespoon of cornstarch to reduce streaking, and 2 cups water. Shake well before using to mix in the cornstarch. Spray on windows and wipe dry. Add essential oils to cover the vinegar smell if desired.

Make a Cleaning List

Better, make a timed cleaning list. This one sounds simplistic. However, if you know what to do, and have it written down, you don't get sidetracked. If you've allowed fifteen minutes to dust, pickup and vacuum the living room, you are much less likely so sit down with one of the magazines you are supposed to be putting away. Everyone's list is different, depending on time available and needs. There are many cleaning lists and books out there for reference, but you are the person who knows best what needs to be done regularly in your home.

Hang a Tennis Ball in Your Garage

Our garages have become the new storage areas. This makes it important to know where to park our car, so that we can walk around and find things and so we don't take anything out of the garage with the car. Hang a tennis ball from the garage ceiling to mark when your car should come to a stop. One the tennis ball can touch the hood, you'll know to stop the car and turn off the ignition.

Take Off Your Shoes When You Come in the House

Between 70 and 80 percent of the dirt in your house comes from your feet or your pet's feet. If you get into the habit of wiping your feet well and removing your shoes when you come in the door, that will cut down significantly on the amount of time you spend dusting, vacuuming and sweeping. Consider slipper socks, house shoes or indoor shoes such as clogs.

Have a Quick Cleaning Routine for Last Minute Visitors

It happens to all of us. Our spouse is bringing some one home, or your son's friends are stopping by. Or maybe you just want a quick clean up before sitting down for the night. Whatever the reason, have a "down and dirty" cleaning plan. This is not the time for serious cleaning, this is the time for a quick pick up and dust and bathroom wipe down. Everyone's plan is different, but if every family member knows what to do if, say, John's teacher is coming over in half an hour; life will be much easier over all.

Use a Homemade Car Deodorizer

First clean all the trash out of your car, vacuum and remove floor mats. Mix the deodorizer recipe below. Use a small sieve or colander and sprinkle all over your car seats and floor. Let the deodorizer sit for an hour or more. Vacuum thoroughly and return mats to the car. Recipe: 1 cup baking soda and 3-4 drops of the essential oil of your choice.

Conclusion

I hope this report is helpful to you and gives you many ideas on how to have a wonderfully clean house with less effort, time and money.

The next step is for you to begin using the hacks shared in this report. As you clean your home, try a couple of these hacks in your kitchen, living room or other areas. You'll be surprised and pleased by just how much easier cleaning your home is using these hacks!

Thank you and happy cleaning!

Printed in Great Britain
by Amazon

37692101R00036